# THE BEST of THE
# WORLD'S
# STUPIDEST
# SIGNS

While the majority of these signs were spotted by the Publisher, we would also like to thank those readers who sought out or stumbled upon silly signs of their own. If you see a daft sign or ridiculous instruction that you feel just has to be shared with the world, then please email it to jokes@michaelomarabooks.com and we will endeavour to include it in our next book.

# THE BEST of THE WORLD'S STUPIDEST SIGNS

Michael O'Mara Humour

First published in Great Britain in 2004 by
Michael O'Mara Books Limited
9 Lion Yard, Tremadoc Road
London SW4 7NQ

Parts of this compilation first appeared in *The World's Stupidest Signs* (2000) and *More of the World's Stupidest Signs* (2003)

A CIP catalogue record for this book is available from the British Library

ISBN 1-84317-113-9

1 3 5 7 9 10 8 6 4 2

Designed and typeset by Design 23

Printed and bound in Great Britain by William Clowes, Beccles, Suffolk

www.mombooks.com

**WEARING THIS GARMENT DOES NOT ENABLE YOU TO FLY**

On a child's Superman costume

# ICE CREAM TOILETS

**On a campsite**

# WE DO NOT TEAR YOUR CLOTHING WITH MACHINERY. WE DO IT CAREFULLY BY HAND.

**In a dry-cleaner's**

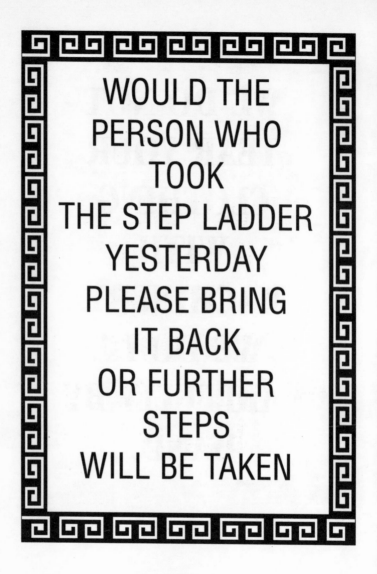

WOULD THE
PERSON WHO
TOOK
THE STEP LADDER
YESTERDAY
PLEASE BRING
IT BACK
OR FURTHER
STEPS
WILL BE TAKEN

**In a factory**

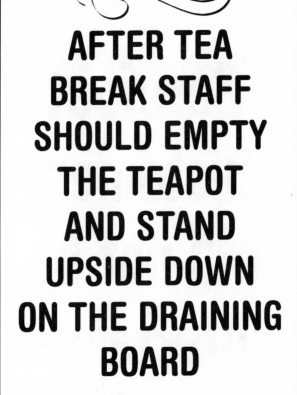

AFTER TEA
BREAK STAFF
SHOULD EMPTY
THE TEAPOT
AND STAND
UPSIDE DOWN
ON THE DRAINING
BOARD

**In an office**

# Barefoot customers will not be entertained

**In the cinema at Rotorua,
New Zealand**

We will sell gasoline to anyone in a glass container

**At an American gas station**

# Mothers, Please Wash Your Hans Before Eating

**English sign in a German café**

# THE TOWN HALL, IS CLOSED UNTIL OPENING. IT WILL REMAIN CLOSED AFTER BEING OPENED. OPEN TOMORROW

Sign outside a new town hall,
which was to be opened by
the Prince of Wales

**SLOW CATTLE CROSSING NO OVERTAKING FOR THE NEXT 100 YRS**

Seen at the side of a British road

ONE HOUR
PHOTOS
READY
IN 20
MINUTES

**Outside a shop in London**

# SAFETY FIRST PLEASE PUT ON YOUR SEAT BELT PREPARE FOR ACCIDENT

Sign in a Japanese taxi

**SWIMMING POOL SUGGESTIONS**
**OPEN 24 HOURS**
**LIFEGUARD ON DUTY**
**8AM TO 8PM**
**DROWNING ABSOLUTELY PROHIBITED**

**Sign at a resort in the Philippines**

# WE CAN REPAIR ANYTHING.

**(PLEASE KNOCK HARD
ON THE DOOR –
THE BELL
DOESN'T WORK)**

Sign on a repair-shop door

# TOILET OUT OF ORDER PLEASE USE FLOOR BELOW

**In a toilet in a London office block**

# OPEN SEVEN DAYS A WEEK

**(EXCEPT MONDAYS)**

**Sign at a New York restaurant**

# PLEASE DO NOT LEAN ON THE WIDOW

On a cruise ship

WANTED
UNMARRIED
GIRLS
TO PICK FRESH
FRUIT
AND PRODUCE
AT NIGHT

On a farm

**In an American maternity ward**

# FOR INDOOR OR OUTDOOR USE ONLY

**On a string of Chinese-made Christmas lights**

# SMARTS IS THE MOST EXCLUSIVE DISCO IN TOWN EVERYONE WELCOME

**Outside a disco**

# WARNING
## Footpath Unsuitable for Pedestrians

# Don't let your worries kill you. Let the church help.

Sign outside a church in the USA

# WE UNBLOCK YOUR CONSTIPATION WITH OUR FINGERS

**Ad for an American reflexology clinic**

DUE TO
INCREASING
PROBLEMS
WITH LITTER LOUTS
AND VANDALS
WE MUST ASK
ANYONE WITH
RELATIVES
BURIED IN THE
GRAVEYARD
TO DO THEIR BEST
TO KEEP THEM IN
ORDER

**Notice sent to residents of an
English village**

**ELEPHANTS PLEASE STAY IN YOUR CAR**

In a safari park

# GOOD APPEARANCE PLEASE

# NO

# WATERMELON PLEASE

**Sign in a Beijing hotel lobby**

# BARGAIN BASEMENT UPSTAIRS

**Sign in a London department store**

# SALE OF LOST AND UNCLAIMED PROPERTY

## UMBRELLAS BY THE THOUSAND, HANDBAGS, BRIEFCASES, OVERCOATS, ABANDONED CHILDREN

**Advert from lost-property auction guide**

# DO NOT

## DRIVE CAR OR OPERATE MACHINERY

**On a bottle of children's cough medicine**

# WE EXCHANGE ANYTHING

## BICYCLES, WASHING MACHINES ETC WHY NOT BRING YOUR WIFE ALONG AND GET A WONDERFUL BARGAIN?

Outside a second-hand shop

# HORSE MANURE

## 50p PER PRE-PACKED BAG

## 20p DO-IT-YOURSELF

**Outside a farm**

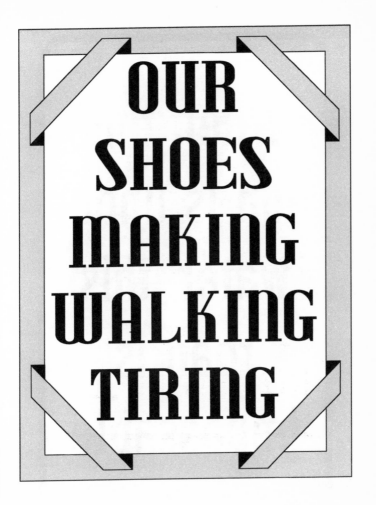

**Advert for a Jakarta shoe company**

# When this sign is under water, this road is impassable

**On a Tennessee highway**

# AUTOMATIC WASHING MACHINES

## PLEASE REMOVE ALL YOUR CLOTHES WHEN THE LIGHT GOES OUT

**Sign in a launderette**

SUITABLE
FOR
VEGETARIANS

**On a bottle of supermarket
mineral water**

# THIS DOOR IS NOT TO BE USED AS AN EXIT OR AN ENTRANCE

**Sign at a New York post office**

# NO
## TRESPASSING
## WITHOUT
## PERMISSION

**Sign on church property**

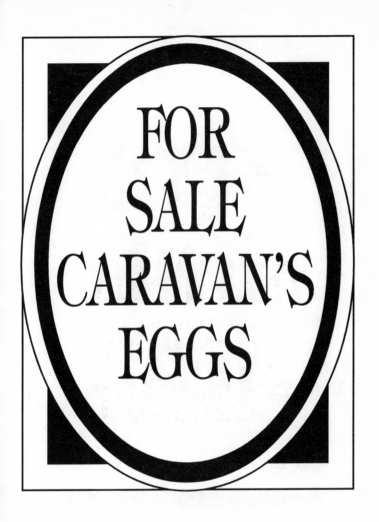

# FOR
# SALE
# CARAVAN'S
# EGGS

**By an English roadside**

# FITS ONE HEAD

**On a shower cap provided by a hotel**

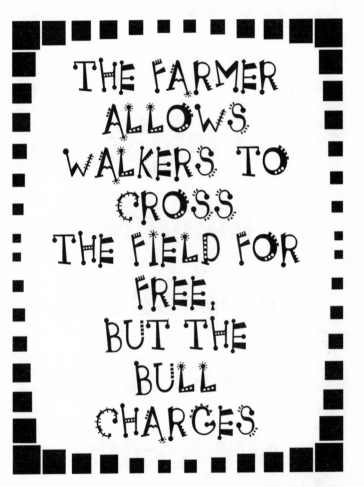

THE FARMER
ALLOWS
WALKERS TO
CROSS
THE FIELD FOR
FREE,
BUT THE
BULL
CHARGES

**Notice in a field**

# Anyone caught hanging from the rim will be suspended

At a basketball court

# FOR ANYONE WHO HAS CHILDREN AND DOESN'T KNOW IT, THERE IS A CRECHE ON THE FIRST FLOOR

**Sign at a conference**

# SAME DAY

# DRY CLEANING

# ALL

# GARMENTS

# READY IN

# 48 HOURS

**In the window of a dry-cleaner's**

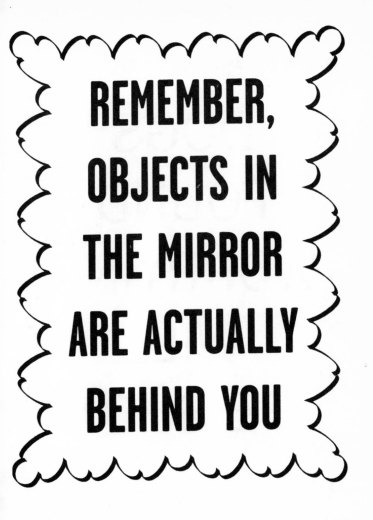

# REMEMBER, OBJECTS IN THE MIRROR ARE ACTUALLY BEHIND YOU

On a helmet-mounted mirror used by US cyclists

DOGS FOUND WORRYING WILL BE SHOT

**Sign on a farm gate**

# USE REPEATEDLY FOR SEVERE DAMAGE

**On a Taiwanese shampoo**

# LOW
# SELF ESTEEM
# SUPPORT GROUP
# MEETS THURSDAY
# AT 7PM

### PLEASE USE
### THE BACK DOOR

**Sign in church hall**

# THIS PRODUCT NOT TESTED ON ANIMALS

**On a New Zealand insect spray**

NO
WALKING,
SITTING
OR
PLAYING ON
THE GRASS
IN THIS
PLEASURE
PARK

**Notice in a London park**

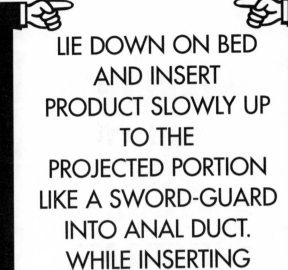

LIE DOWN ON BED
AND INSERT
PRODUCT SLOWLY UP
TO THE
PROJECTED PORTION
LIKE A SWORD-GUARD
INTO ANAL DUCT.
WHILE INSERTING
PRODUCT
FOR APPROXIMATELY
5 MINUTES,
KEEP QUIET

**On a Japanese product used to
relieve painful hemorrhoids**

WE REPAIR
WHAT
YOUR
HUSBAND
FIXED

**Sign on a repair-shop door**

# Monster
# Man
# Eating
# Shark

**At a zoo**

**Manure Please Drive In**

Outside a farm

**Outside an American service station**

YOU HAVE
NO REASON
TO TRY
OUR
BEST
RESTAURANT

**Sign in an Indonesian
hotel restaurant**

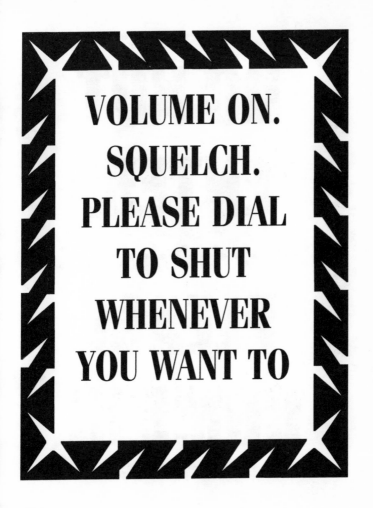

VOLUME ON.
SQUELCH.
PLEASE DIAL
TO SHUT
WHENEVER
YOU WANT TO

**Sign in a Tokyo hotel bathroom**

# DO NOT ENTER.

# PLEASE COME IN.

**Signs on a door at a motel in America**

SEAFOOD
BROUGHT IN
BY CUSTOMERS
WILL NOT BE
ENTERTAINED

**Sign at a restaurant in Malaysia**

## NON-SMOKING FORBIDDEN

**Sign in hotel lobby, Jordan**

# IT IS ADVISORY TO BE TWO PEOPLE DURING ASSEMBLY

**Instructions included with a Swedish flat-packed cabinet**

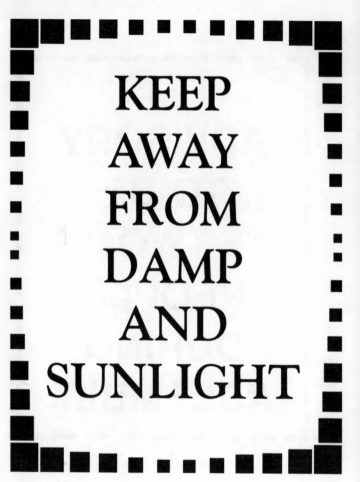

# KEEP AWAY FROM DAMP AND SUNLIGHT

**On a set of garden furniture**

PRIZE
WINNING
HANDMADE
SAUSAGES.
ONCE TASTED
YOU'LL
NEVER
WANT
ANOTHER.

Sign at a farm shop

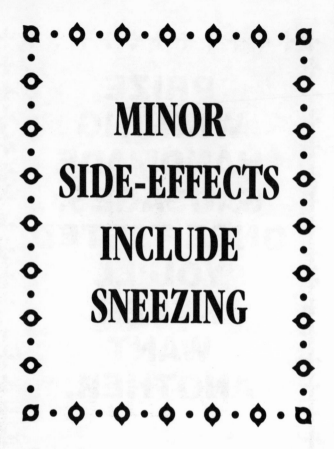

# MINOR SIDE-EFFECTS INCLUDE SNEEZING

**Safety warning on
hay fever nasal-spray remedy**

# ANTIQUE TABLES MADE DAILY

**Sign by a roadside in America**

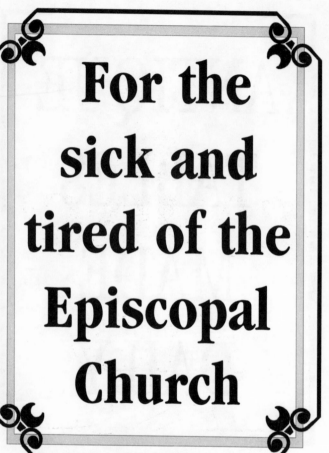

# For the sick and tired of the Episcopal Church

**On a New York convalescent home**

# JESUS
# IS
# COMING!

## NO BINGO
## ON SUNDAY

**Notice outside a US church**

# CAUTION:
## WATER ON
## ROAD
## DURING RAIN

American road sign

# In case of fire, please pay bill promptly

**In a café in Cambridge, England**

Be careful!
Goats like
to nibble
at your
clothes
and butt

At a petting zoo

**NOTICE – PUBLIC BAR**

**Our public bar is presently not open because it is closed**

**Manager**

Outside a bar in Africa

fifteen men's wool suits, £50. They won't last an hour.

In a gentleman's shop

# DANGER PLEASE KEEP OUT

**Sign seen on a litter bin**

# In event of air attack drive off bridge

On the Triborough Bridge
in New York

Toilet →

Stay in
your car

# Parking for Drive-Thru Service Only

At a burger bar in the USA

# Danger Ahead Fasten Safety Belts And Remove Dentures

**Sign near a river in Europe**

# Animals Drive Very Slowly

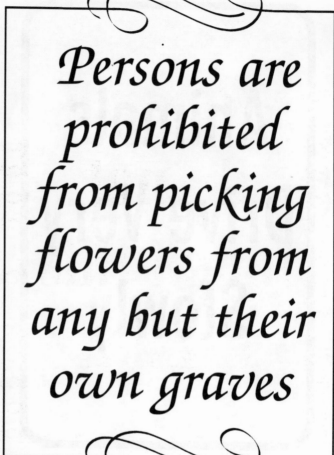

*Persons are prohibited from picking flowers from any but their own graves*

**In a Pennsylvania cemetery**

Braille sign at a museum in London

# PLANTS PRODUCE FLOWERS

In a country lane near Horsham,
England

# Open seven days a week and weekends

In a restaurant

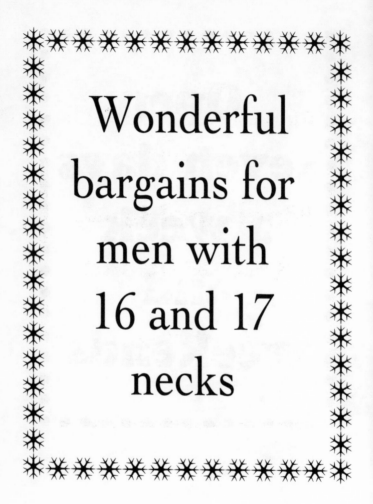

Wonderful bargains for men with 16 and 17 necks

**In a clothing store**

**MAYDAY**
**Please do not smash our windows.**

**Macdonalds →**
**← Starbucks**

**For directions, please ask inside**

Sign on a café in London during the May Day anti-capitalist rally, 2001

# Tourist
# Information &
# Travel
# Services
# (T.I.T.S.)

**Sign in Nepal**

This
Month's
Special
NO FUEL

Outside a petrol station in Africa

# TRESPASERS WILL BE SHOT. SURVIVERS WILL BE SHOT AGAIN.

**On farmland**

# All persons (except players) caught collecting balls on this course will be prosecuted and have their balls removed.

**At a golf course**

# Master Baiter

At a fishing-tackle store in the USA

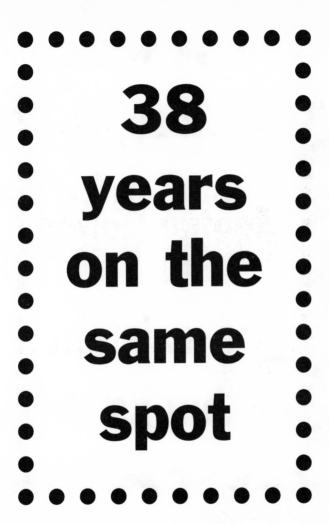

# 38 years on the same spot

**On a long-established
New Mexico drycleaner's**

Rare,
out-of-print
and
non-existent
books

**In an American bookstore**

# Baby and Garage Sale

# Safe for carpets, too!

**On a tin of carpet cleaner**

# No keyboard detected. Press any key to continue.

**Computer error message**

(AMUSEMENTS→) (Toilets)

**Signs in Bournemouth, England**

# Do not put wet clothes in dryers, as this can cause irreparable damage.

**In a launderette**

# DO NOT ACTIVATE WITH WET HANDS

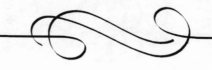

**Sign on a hand-dryer in
a public toilet**

IF BUILDING
IN WHICH
HEATER
RESIDES IS ON
FIRE, DO NOT
GO INTO
BUILDING.

On a gas water heater

# This floodlight is capable of illuminating large areas, even in the dark.

**On a floodlight**

# Planned Parenthood

# -IN THE REAR→

**Outside a family-planning clinic in the USA**

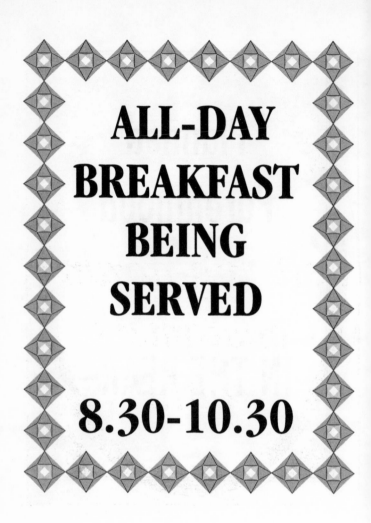

**ALL-DAY BREAKFAST BEING SERVED**

**8.30-10.30**

**In a café**

Toilet
for
sitting-down
customers
only

**In a Scottish tea shop**

# Craft shop left under bridge

**Sign in London**

**Eat What You Like Only £9.95**

**Children Only £2.95**

**In a buffet restaurant**

# DIETING GROUP WILL MEET AT 7PM AT THE FIRST PRESBYTERIAN CHURCH.

PLEASE USE LARGE DOUBLE DOOR
AT THE SIDE ENTRANCE.

**Notice on a church bulletin board**

# TASTES SO GOOD THIS BOX NEVER CLOSES! TO CLOSE: PLACE TAB HERE

**Advertising and instructions on an American cereal packet**

**Notice on Norfolk village shop door**

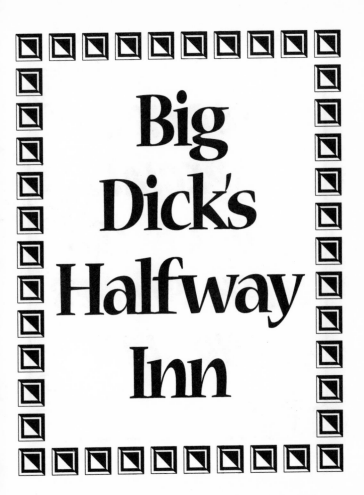

# Big Dick's Halfway Inn

**At a resort in the USA**

TODAY'S
SPECIAL
POT OF TEA
WITH STONES
AND JAM

**Sign in a tea shop**

Do not swim beyond the buoys. No one in the town is expected to save you if you fail to heed this warning.

**Sign in a village on the Black Sea**

**Sign in London pizza restaurant**

**BABY SHOW**

ALL ENTRIES
TO BE
HANDED
IN AT
THE GATE

Sign at a garden fête

**WAITRESSES REQUIRED FOR BREAKFAST**

In a café window

**CUSTOMERS WHO FIND OUR WAITING STAFF RUDE SHOULD SEE THE MANAGER**

In a restaurant

# IF YOU ARE SATISFACTORY PLEASE TELL YOUR FRIENDS IF YOU ARE NOT SATISFACTORY PLEASE TELL THE WAITER

In a Chinese restaurant

TRY OUR
LOCAL BUTTER
NOBODY CAN
TOUCH IT

**In a grocery shop**

**OUR MOTTO:**
**WE PROMISE**
**YOU THE**
**LOWEST**
**PRICES**
**AND**
**WORKMANSHIP**

**Outside a furniture shop**

AUTO
REPAIR
SERVICE.
FREE PICK-UP
AND DELIVERY.
TRY US ONCE,
YOU'LL NEVER
GO ANYWHERE
AGAIN.

**Outside a garage**

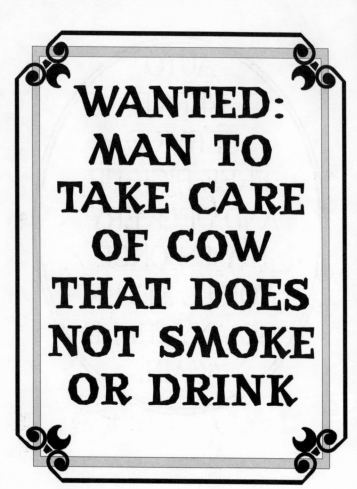

WANTED:
MAN TO
TAKE CARE
OF COW
THAT DOES
NOT SMOKE
OR DRINK

**Sign on a farm**

OUR BIKINIS ARE EXCITING. THEY ARE SIMPLY THE TOPS.

**Advert in a dress-shop window**

*Whole Chicken Medium Fresh*

**From a supermarket leaflet in London**

# Please do not lock the door as we have lost the key.

**In an Irish hotel room**

**In a Mexico City hotel**

# THIS IS THE GATE OF HEAVEN. ENTER YE ALL BY THIS DOOR.

**(THIS DOOR IS KEPT LOCKED BECAUSE OF THE DRAUGHT– PLEASE USE SIDE DOOR.)**

**On a church door**

# Archery Tournament

# Ears Pierced

**Adjacent signs outside a shopping mall**

# CAUTION: AUTOMATIC DOOR PUSH TO OPERATE

**On the entrance door
of an office building**

# QUICKSAND

## ANY PERSON PASSING THIS POINT WILL BE DROWNED
## BY ORDER OF THE DISTRICT COUNCIL

**Sign warning of quicksand**

# NO MUDDY BOOTS PLEASE OR DOGS SMOKING ICE CREAMS

**Sign on the door of a souvenir shop in Porlock Weir, Somerset, England**

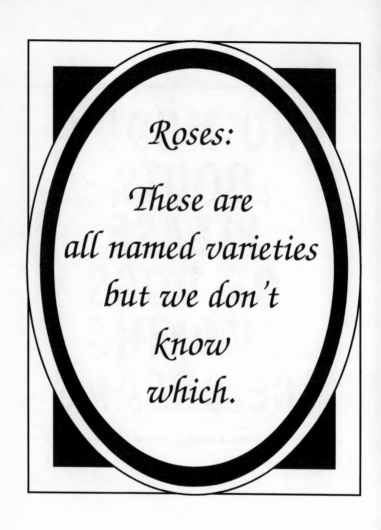

*Roses:*

*These are all named varieties but we don't know which.*

**At a garden centre**

# Now available in multi-packs

**On a display of 'I Love You Only' Valentine cards**

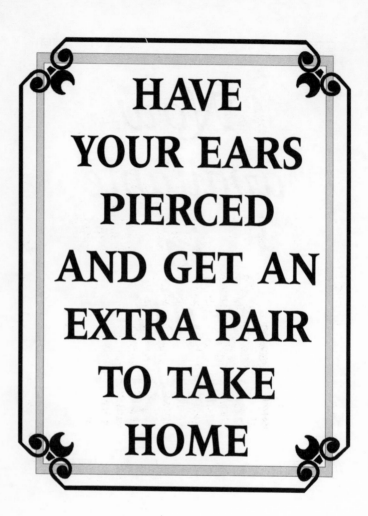

HAVE
YOUR EARS
PIERCED
AND GET AN
EXTRA PAIR
TO TAKE
HOME

**In a jewellery shop**

**CAUTION:
Do not
run on the
stairs.
Use the
handrail.**

Sign at a railway station

# One can peel tomatoes easily by standing in boiling water for a minute.

**In the cookery column of the *Daily Mail***

# Leather Faced Ladies Handbags

**On a market stall**

# No Cycling Dogs On Leads

**PRODUCE OF MORE THAN ONE COUNTRY**

On a SINGLE pre-packaged vanilla pod
in most supermarkets!

**CLOSED DUE TO ILLNESS**

Notice in health-food shop window

# Drive In Car Park

# WARNING:
## DO NOT DRIVE WHILST USING THIS PRODUCT

**On a packet of condoms**

# Remove before driving

On a car windscreen frost cover

# PLEASE MIND THE STEPS

**Outside a dance academy**

*Genuine*

*Faux*

*Pearls*

**In a jewellery store**

# Cup of coffee to sit in or take away

**Outside a coffee shop in
Malvern, England**

# Ask about our plans for owning your home

**In the offices of a loan company**

In the interest of safety, it is advisable to keep your child away from fire & flames

Label on a cot blanket and children's clothing from a famous British high-street store

# Do not pour liquids into your television set

In a TV owner's manual

**USER INSTRUCTIONS:** Remove outer packaging. Wash with soap in warm water to form lather.

Rinse off and dry.

On a bar of soap

# 100% pure all-natural fresh-squeezed orange juice from concentrate

On a carton of orange juice

# STYLIST WANTED.

GOOD PAY AND FRINGE BENEFITS. EXCELLENT GROWTH POTENTIAL.

**Notice in hairdresser's window**

# Restricted to unauthorized personnel

**At a number of British military bases**

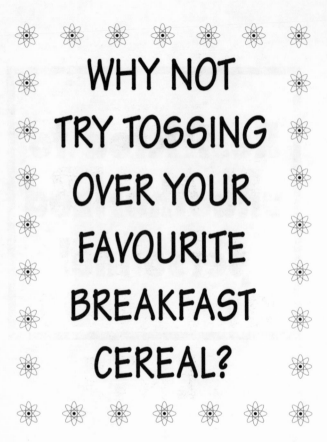

# WHY NOT TRY TOSSING OVER YOUR FAVOURITE BREAKFAST CEREAL?

On a packet of raisins

# NOW IS THE SUMMER OF OUR DISCOUNT TENTS

In the window of a camping shop
in Bolton, England

# Able to do the worst possible job

**Sign in a dry-cleaner's**

Does your child wet the bed? Enquire within.

**Sign outside a chemist's shop in Liverpool in the 1960s**

# ♟ Michael O'Mara Humour